# Zion's
## Amazing Encounter with The Great King!

**Evangelist Jahne' Mitchell**

Text Copyright © 2025 by Evangelist Jahne' Mitchell

Photo Credits: The Mitchell Family

Illustrations Copyright: SUSU Entertainment LLC

All rights reserved. No part of this publication may be reproduced, distributed, or transmitted in any form or by any means, including photocopying, recording, or other electronic or mechanical methods without the prior written permission of the publisher.

SUSU Entertainment LLC
P.O. Box 1621
Cypress, TX 77410
Website: www.susuentertainmentllc.com
Email: susuentertainmentllc@gmail.com

Printed in the United States of America

Name: Evangelist Jahne' Mitchell, Author

Title: Zion's Amazing Encounter with The Great King!

Summary: A heartwarming story of a little girl entering school for the very first time. She feels nervous and out of place. Everyone seems to have a friend except her, and the days start to feel long and lonely. She receives a gentle reminder from her parents and brothers, something powerful: God is always with you. Young readers will understand that faith can bring comfort, courage, and even unexpected friendships.

Identifiers:
ISBN: 978-1-956292-40-4 (hardcover)
ISBN: 978-1-956292-41-1 (paperback)

Subject: God's Love | Family Support | True Friendships

Book Cover Design © 2025 by SUSU Entertainment LLC

# Dedication

This book is lovingly dedicated to...

My Heavenly Father, who calls me, equips me, and carries me daily. Thank you for choosing me for this work and for being my constant source of strength, wisdom and peace.

My husband, Michael T. Mitchell, Jr., my rock and greatest encourager. Thank you for believing in me, covering me in prayer, and walking beside me through every season. I could not do this without your love and support.

My children, Caleb, Aaron, Noah and Zion, my heartbeats and my greatest earthly blessings. You are the reason I strive to grow, to speak life, and to follow God's purpose for my life. May you always know how loved, seen, and anointed you are and that the Great King Jesus is always with you.

To every parent, guardian and child reading this, this is for you. May you find healing, strength, and encouragement within these pages. You matter. Your story matters, and God is not finished with you yet.

May this book remind you that God is always present, always working, and always writing a beautiful story through you, for you, and for his glory.


With all my love,
Evangelist Jahne' Mitchell

# Introduction

Starting school is a big adventure - full of new faces, unfamiliar places, and sometimes, big feelings. This is the story of a little girl named Zion Grace who bravely steps into her very first classroom, hoping to find a friend but feeling all alone. As the days go by, she begins to wonder if she will ever find a friend, but when the world feels quiet and lonely, her parents remind her of a special truth: *God, The Great King is always with you, even when you feel alone*. With that comfort in her heart, something beautiful begins to change.

This story is about friendship, faith, and the quiet ways that love finds us - especially when we need it most. It's for every child who has ever felt left out, and for every parent who has whispered a prayer over a little one's first big steps. Because sometimes, all it takes is one friend... and the reminder that you're never alone.

Once upon a time a beautiful girl named Zion Grace was born. She had the most sparkling eyes you could imagine.

Zion was the only girl among three older brothers: Caleb, Aaron, and Noah.

Zion's parents always reminded their children of how special they were, teaching them that they belonged to God and were loved beyond measure.
They would often say to Zion, "You are beautiful, smart, and you belong to God." Their parents made sure that they knew that their family was centered around their faith and identity in God.

**Every night, they would gather to pray and read from the Bible, always reiterating to Zion and her brothers of God's promises.**

Four years had passed, when one beautiful and sunny day, Zion woke up with excitement because it was her 5th birthday!

The house was buzzing with joy as balloons and streamers filled every corner. Zion's birthday party was a day full of fun, delicious food and cake, exciting games, lots of candy, and presents wrapped with love.

Big brothers, Caleb, Aaron, and Noah joined in on the fun, making her laugh and play all day long.

The following year, it was time for Zion to start school. She felt a mixture of excitement and worry. She asked her older brothers, "Will I be okay at school?" Caleb, Aaron, and Noah reassured her, "You'll do just fine, Zion."

The brothers showered her with a snug hug. "We know that you are brave and smart!" Although her brothers calmed her down, Zion still felt nervous. She was used to being at home with her family, and the idea of going to school made her tummy feel all twisty.

"What if the other kids aren't as nice as you guys?" Zion asked her Mommy and Daddy. They hugged her and said, "Remember, God is with you always, no matter where you go."

Every morning before school, Zion's mommy and daddy would pray with her. They reminded her of the Bible verse from Joshua 1:9, "Be strong and courageous. Do not be frightened, and do not be dismayed, for the Lord your God is with you wherever you go."

Despite their comforting words, Zion still had many questions about God. She wondered how he looked and if he was really there with her. Her mommy and daddy encouraged her to always trust and believe in God's promises.

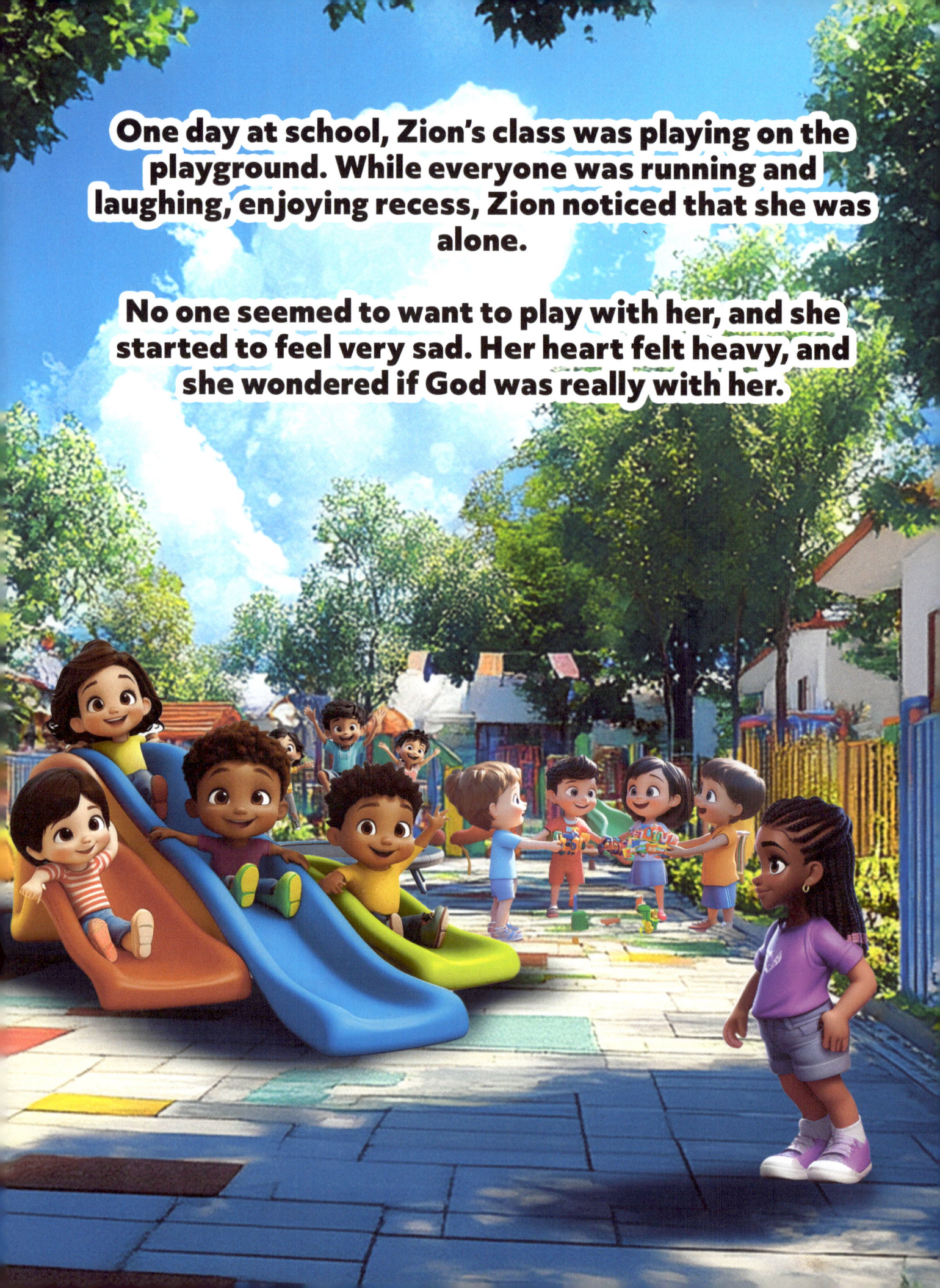

One day at school, Zion's class was playing on the playground. While everyone was running and laughing, enjoying recess, Zion noticed that she was alone.

No one seemed to want to play with her, and she started to feel very sad. Her heart felt heavy, and she wondered if God was really with her.

**Suddenly, Zion felt a warm, comforting presence around her, as if a gentle breeze was wrapping her in a hug. She felt a surge of joy and peace that she had never experienced before. It seemed God was giving her a special, invisible hug, letting her know she wasn't alone.**

Tears of happiness rolled down Zion's cheeks as she realized that God was indeed with her. Her teacher, Mrs. McDonald, noticed Zion crying and came over to check on her.

Mrs. McDonald asked, "Zion, are you okay?" Zion looked up with a big smile and said, "These are tears of joy because I know that my God is with me. He is the Great King!" Mrs. McDonald smiled back and gave Zion a comforting pat on the back.

Zion felt a new strength and confidence as she stood up from the swing. She was ready to face the rest of the day, knowing she had God's love surrounding her.

The next day, something wonderful happened. A new student named Amelia joined the class. Amelia had a friendly smile and a kind heart. Zion and Amelia quickly became friends.

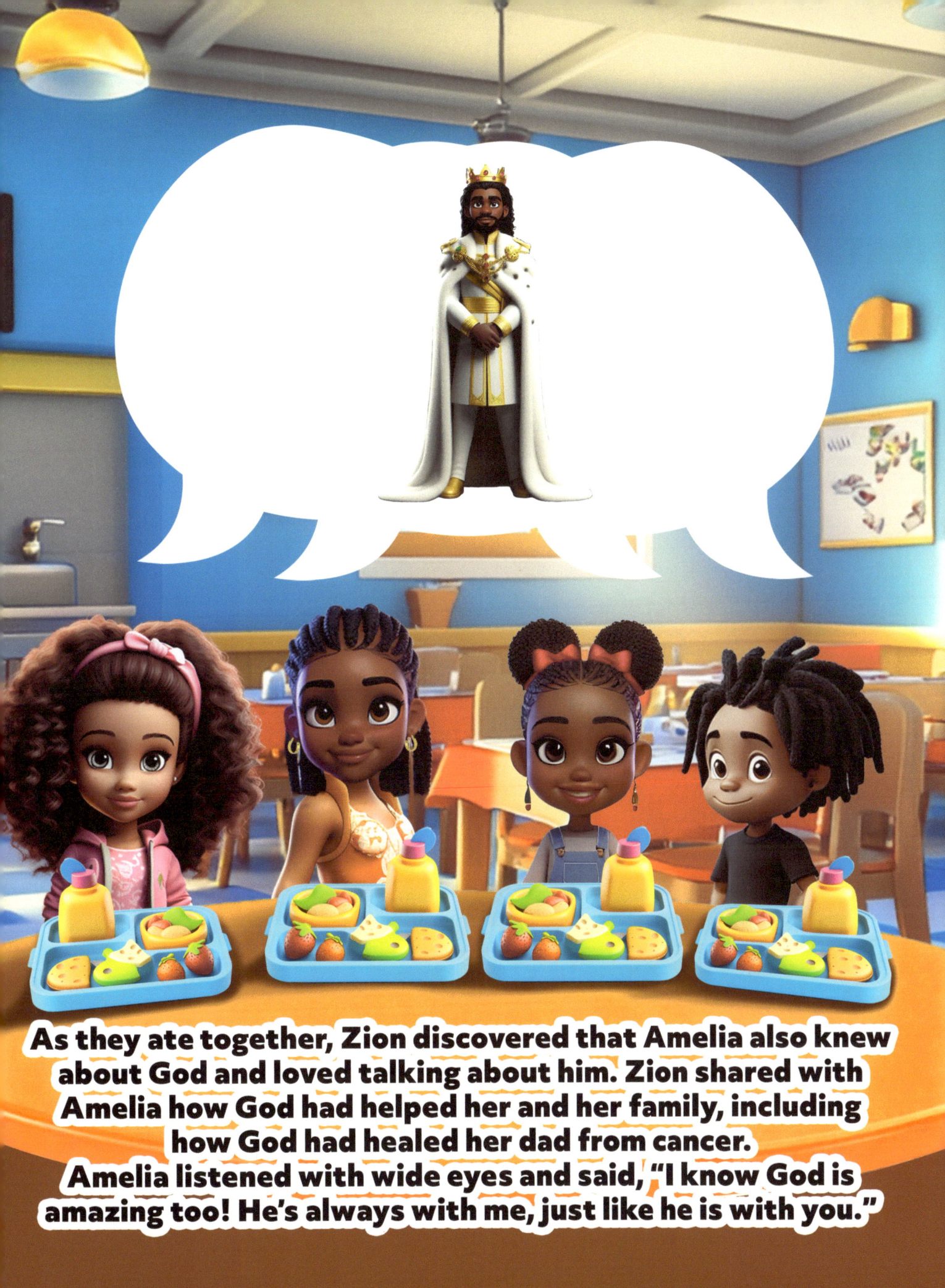

As they ate together, Zion discovered that Amelia also knew about God and loved talking about him. Zion shared with Amelia how God had helped her and her family, including how God had healed her dad from cancer.
Amelia listened with wide eyes and said, "I know God is amazing too! He's always with me, just like he is with you."

Zion and Amelia became the best of friends. They spent their days playing and talking about God's love and his incredible power. They knew that with God on their side, they could face anything together. At school, they would encourage each other with Bible verses and share their favorite stories from the Bible. It felt wonderful to have a friend who understood and loved God just like she did.

One day, during a class project, Zion and Amelia worked together to build a beautiful model of a garden. As they worked, they talked about how God made everything so wonderful and he was always there to guide them.

They remembered another Bible verse from Psalm 139:7, "Where can I go from your Spirit? Where can I flee from your presence?" They laughed, knowing that there was nowhere they could go where God wasn't with them.

Zion and Amelia's friendship grew stronger with each passing day. They supported each other through homework, shared their favorite stories, and celebrated each other's successes. Zion felt blessed to have found such a special friend.

Zion and Amelia both knew that their friendship was a gift from God, and they thanked him for bringing them together. They prayed together before school each day, asking God to help them be kind and loving to everyone.

Zion's family was thrilled to hear about her new friend Amelia and the joy she found at school. Mommy and Daddy were proud of how Zion was growing in her faith and learning to trust God in every situation.

They continued their family talks and Bible studies, making sure Zion and her brothers stayed close to God.

# Praying 4 Our Kidz

Zion's mommy even started a podcast called "Praying 4 Our Kidz" to help nurture families through the word of God and prayer. Zion knew that her family's love and guidance were important, but she also felt a special bond with God that made her feel secure and loved.

One evening, as Zion was getting ready for bed, she reflected on her day with Amelia. She thanked God for her new friend and for helping her through her fears. Zion's heart was full of gratitude, knowing that God had been with her every step of the way.

Mommy read the Bible, reminding her of another comforting verse, Isaiah 41:10: "So do not fear, for I am with you; do not be dismayed, for I am your God." Zion snuggled into her covers, feeling safe and cherished.

**Mommy tucked Zion in as she started getting sleepy, thinking about all the wonderful things God had done for her. She was grateful for her family, her friends, and most importantly, for God's never-ending love and presence in her life.**

She thought about adventures with her new friend Amelia and felt a sense of peace, knowing that God, the Great King, was always with her.
Zion knew that no matter where life took her, she could face it with courage and joy because of God's love.

And so, Zion's days were filled with joy, peace, happiness and faith. She learned that God was always with her, whether she was playing on the playground, working on school projects, or spending time with her family and friends.

With God by her side, Zion knew she could overcome any challenge and enjoy every blessing. Zion and Amelia's friendship grew stronger, and they continued to support each other with love and prayers. Together, they discovered the true joy of knowing that God, The Great King was with them every step of the way.

**GOD THE GREAT KING LOVES YOU!**

# Acknowledgements

To God be the glory, for the great things He has done. First and foremost, I give all honor and glory to God. Without Him, I am nothing. He is the source of my strength, the giver of every good gift, and the reason this book exists. Every word within these pages is a reflection of His love and faithfulness.

To my loving husband, Michael T. Mitchell, Jr., thank you for everything you do for our family and for standing beside me as I pursue the dreams God has placed in my heart. Your encouragement, sacrifice, and unwavering support means more than words could ever express.

To my precious children, Caleb, Aaron, Noah and Zion, you are my greatest treasures. Your lives inspire every prayer, every page, and every purpose behind this work. You are the living proof of God's goodness.

To my church family at Perfecting Holiness Non-Denominational Church, under the great leadership of Bishop Wiley Thornton III and Overseer Yolanda Thornton. Thank you for your spiritual covering, your love, and your leadership. PHNC is more than a church, it is a place where lives are transformed and purpose is birth.

Thank you to all our family and friends for your continuous love and support.

A special thank you to our "Praying for Our Kidz" community and all the incredible families connected to it. Your faithful presence, prayers and support have helped us reach across nations with the healing power of God's word. Whether you've joined us live or listened to the Facebook podcast replay, your commitment has made an international impact. Thank you for showing up. Thank you for standing in the gap for our children.

A great appreciation to our book publishers with SUSU Entertainment LLC for your guidance and support throughout our literary journey.

This book is a labor of love birth in prayer, lived through faith and written with purpose. May it continue to shine light, bring hope, and glorify God in every way.

# About The Author

I'm Evangelist Jahne' Mitchell, Minister of the Gospel, wife, mom, business owner and someone who loves Jesus with all my heart. I started writing because I wanted children and families to know that God is always with them no matter what they're facing. Many of my stories come straight from my own life, especially moments with my children. I believe God speaks to us every day in every way whether you are going through good or bad times. My hope is that every page helps families get a closer relationship with God and be open to the plan and purpose He has for your life.

One of my favorite scriptures is Romans 8:28; "And we know that all things work together for good to those who love God, to those who are called according to his purpose." I truly believe that, and I want you to believe it too.

# The Mitchell Family

Contact Evangelist Jahne' Mitchell:

<u>Facebook</u>
@kingdom.kidz.adventures

<u>Email</u>
**kingdomkidzadventures101@gmail.com**

<u>Facebook</u>
Praying For Our Kidz Virtual Ministry

www.ingramcontent.com/pod-product-compliance
Lightning Source LLC
Chambersburg PA
CBHW041411010526
44107CB00015B/1135